WONDERS OF
ANIMAL NURSERIES

Jacquelyn Berrill

ILLUSTRATED BY THE AUTHOR

DODD, MEAD & COMPANY, NEW YORK

To those who filled our nursery with laughter
that still echoes in my heart

Contents

1

Animal Nurseries

A nursery is a place where young animals are kept safe and warm
and well fed until they grow strong enough to take care of themselves. Sometimes the nurseries are found in strange places, but
each animal acts according to its kind. The robins always build
the same kind of nests in the same places each year; the same
tree holes house a new generation of raccoons each season. The
rabbit makes its nursery in a field not far from where it had once
found warmth and food, and the chipmunk baby knows only an
underground nursery. The tiger cub feels perfectly at home in a
rock den.

Many nurseries are more exposed. The bat, for instance, must
cling to its mother as she zooms through the air catching insects,
for even this is safer than hanging alone in the cave.

Many creatures hide only while the baby is being born. Some,
like the camel, have to keep up with the mother and the herd
almost at once. And so the kind of nursery depends on the help-
lessness of the baby—and the length of time a nursery is needed
also depends on the amount of time needed for the mother or
parents to teach the young how to find their own food and protect themselves from their enemies.

Much that animals do may be just instinct, but even the long
play periods that some creatures have are very important learning
sessions. As the lion cubs wrestle and spring and pounce, they
learn to be hunters. All young animals have to know the laws of

nature and it is in the nursery and during the time they are with their parents that they learn these lessons or they do not live long.

Let's take a look at the nursery life of some of our well-known animals.

A warbler feeds her young

2

Bird Nurseries

Bird parents are very much concerned about their precious eggs, and because birds have wings and generally live in the branches of trees when they are not actually flying, this is where most of them raise their young. They have to build nests that will keep their eggs and babies from falling to the ground.

Usually the female builds the nest; sometimes both birds build it. But each kind of bird makes the best nest possible for laying its eggs in it.

Birds have warm bodies and usually need to sit upon their eggs and nestlings most of the time to keep them warm enough to hatch and grow. Most young birds, when they first hatch, are naked and helpless and so have to be warmed and fed by their parents for a long time before they can take care of themselves.

The bird's nest in a tree may swing wildly in the breezes, but it is a relatively safe nursery compared to those on Antarctic ice or on rafts in a swift-flowing stream or high up on a cliff above the ocean. Yet all bird parents have the same idea—that of caring for their eggs and fledglings until the young birds are able to take care of themselves.

EMPEROR PENGUIN

It would be hard to think of a stranger nursery than one on the Antarctic ice pack, near the South Pole, with temperatures reach-

9

ing seventy degrees below zero. But it is under just such conditions that the emperor penguin female lays her one precious egg. Perhaps the reason penguins choose the dark, cold mid-winter for their breeding time is the same reason why our woodland animals have their babies in the early spring and not in the summer: so they can have a long time to grow before winter comes. With penguins it is important for the babies to grow big enough to have the kind of feathers they need before the next winter, and so they must hatch when they do to give the fledglings time to grow up.

Emperor penguins are large birds that stand four feet high and weigh about ninety pounds. Both the male and female wear the same "formal suits"; indeed, we can't tell them apart as they walk slowly and with great dignity about on the ice. They are able to walk upright because their feet are set farther back than in most birds. The greater part of their lives is spent in water, where they seem to fly through the waves instead of swimming. Yes, the water is very cold, but penguins have short stiff feathers that

A penguin tucks the egg into its warm nursery

overlap in such a way that no moisture can get through, so they don't feel the cold at all.

In July, in the dark, cold, mid-winter of the Antarctic, the emperor penguins come together in breeding colonies, called rookeries. On the ice there is nothing with which to make nests, so each female lays her one white egg, which weighs about a pound, on top of her webbed feet. She covers it with a fold of skin on her abdomen, which is almost like having it in a pouch.

Both parents take turns keeping the egg warm in their feather-lined nurseries, and when they change it from one warm nursery pouch to the other, it must be done without letting the egg touch the ice. One contact with the cold ice and the chick would die!

You can imagine how still the parent who is nursing the egg has to stay. The new chick hatches after seven or eight weeks, and is naked and helpless. It is several more days before it is covered with soft down, but it stays all cuddled in the feather fold and only sticks its head out to be fed. When feeding, it puts its head into the parent's mouth, way down into the throat, where the food is transferred to the baby chick.

The baby seems to grow slowly, but after a while the fluffy fledgling feathers make it look larger than the parent. It still tries to cuddle in the nursery fold. When the chick is six months old, it molts, and this time grows a suit of formal dress like the parents, complete with orange tie, for every adult emperor penguin has some vivid orange feathers on each side of its neck. From now on, the chick can go into the water and swim about like its parents, catching fish.

GREBE

Most birds that spend their lives on the water leave it to make their nurseries on dry land, usually on rocks or sand, but the grebe, a close relative of the loon, makes a floating raft of the

Grebe on its raft nest

buoyant stems of water plants and attaches it to reeds so that it won't drift away. She lays her eggs in a slight depression in the center, and when she leaves the nest she carefully covers it with leaves and reeds so that it will look like just a mass of floating brush.

Since grebes are found on many ponds and lakes all across America, perhaps you can find such a floating nursery, rocked gently by the waves. If you look closely, you may see the mother bird hiding in the water, with only her eyes and bill above the surface watching for her enemies, the hunter and the hawk. Or you may be lucky enough to see her swimming along with one of her babies on her back, hitching a ride because it has become too tired to swim any farther.

MURRE

Murres, sea birds that look somewhat like penguins in their black and white "formal dress," arrive by the hundreds each spring to nest on some of the rocky cliffs along the Atlantic coast.

*Murres lay their pointed
egg on a cliff ledge*

One can hardly say they nest, for the nursery of the murre chick is a bare rock on a cliff ledge a hundred feet up, where each pair of birds lays its single egg and stands guard over it.

You may wonder why the eggs don't roll off and break on the rocks below, but nature has taken care of this. These sea birds lay eggs that are pointed at one end; when they roll, they pivot in a circle without rolling away. Marvelous, isn't it?

Each pair of murres watches over the single chick and feeds it carefully, and when the baby is two or three weeks old, the family—parents and chick—fly off together to the open sea, where the young finishes growing.

13

3

Tree Nurseries

SQUIRREL

Other animals besides birds build their nurseries in treetops where their young can be safely hidden in the thick leaves or in holes in the tree trunks. Perhaps you have squirrel nurseries in your garden trees. They may be the friendly gray squirrels, with frisky, graceful tails, or the small nervous red squirrels that leap from branch to branch, or the shy flying squirrels that glide about in the evening.

The rusty red squirrel may have a den in a tree hole or live in a nest of leaves and twigs high up in the tree. You can hear his loud chattering as he fusses at another squirrel who comes too near the nest.

The mother red squirrel sometimes hangs a curtain of moss over the entrance to her nest, and if we could peep behind it, we might see her four or five naked babies snugly asleep inside. They are about four inches from the tip of the tail to the wee nose, and you wouldn't think them very beautiful. However, after ten days they have on coats of very fine fur and begin to look like their parents. The mother stays close to guard them from harm and to nurse them often. When they are six weeks old they come out of their nursery and travel along the limbs near the treetops.

Now they are beautiful, about one-third the size of their mother, and as quick as lightning in their movements.

Red squirrel—mother and young

If at any time the mother feels the nest is unsafe she takes a baby by the loose skin on its stomach and, with its tiny legs and tail curled about its neck, she carries the youngster to a safe place. She leaps from branch to branch with her precious load and then returns for another baby.

The babies learn soon to eat green tree buds and to lick the sweet tree sap, and so they are gradually weaned.

Perhaps you see the red squirrels oftener in the fall, when they are busy preparing for winter, for they store seeds and nuts in their winter homes, and sometimes place mushrooms way up in the treetop for an extra special tidbit.

When the trees are bare of leaves you'll spot numerous nests that look like giant birds' nests. These are the nurseries of the gray squirrels, and in the early spring there are small helpless babies curled up inside the nests.

15

The gray squirrel babies develop very slowly, and their eyes stay closed for the first five weeks. They are about two months old before they venture from their leaf nests or from their nursery homes in a tree hole, and walk about the branches, eating tree flowers and buds. But not long after that, they are running about everywhere, enjoying all kinds of seeds and berries.

Gray squirrels are seen early in the morning

You may see the youngsters almost every morning and late afternoon, for they are very active during those hours, playing and eating. These young gray squirrels are not full-sized until they are two years old, and they spend their first winter with their mother in the tree nest.

My favorite squirrel is the kind that flies, the flying squirrel! These squirrels do not fly like birds, but glide through space from high up in a tree top. They leap into the air, spreading their four legs so that their "wings," which are folds of loose skin along their sides, between the front and back legs, are stretched. Then down they go, turning and twisting by changing the slack in their "wings," and steering with their flat tails. When they are ready to land, their tails go up straight and they turn so they are facing upward, in order to be all ready to run quickly up the tree to get the height needed for the next glide.

Flying squirrels are smaller than their gray and red relatives; when full-grown they are only about a foot long, including their tail, and weigh about four ounces. They have brown fur, which becomes light on the underside, and very large eyes, for they are animals of the night. In fact, they never leave their nests until it is nearly dark, and that is why few people ever see them.

When a pair of flying squirrels is house-hunting, they look for a hole made by a woodpecker, clear out the old nest, fix up a clean one of their own, and move in.

When the babies are born the father moves to a hole nearby and does not interfere with the new family, but remains close enough to help protect them if an enemy approaches.

The babies are very tiny, about half an ounce in weight, and naked, blind, and deaf. After two weeks they start to get their soft, fine, fur coat which they change for a coarse one like their parents' in the fall. The mother rarely leaves them but stands over them, nursing them very often. After five weeks she starts to wean them and so she leaves them for longer periods of time while she hunts food for her fast growing young.

Like other forest mothers, the flying squirrel will fight any enemy who comes too close; and if she feels her babies are not safe in the nursery, she rolls each one in turn in a ball and carries it by the loose skin on its stomach to a safer home. She climbs with her load to the treetop and glides to another tree, runs quickly up that and glides again until she feels it is safe. Then she returns for another baby.

Next time you go to the woods, look for a dead tree with a small hole near the top, rap on the trunk, and maybe you will waken some wee sleepy flying squirrels. They are both friendly and curious and not at all afraid to look out at you.

Flying squirrels look out from their nursery

Raccoon baby

RACCOON

It is in early spring, when the soft air is filled with the perfume of wild flowers and the song of birds, that the little raccoon babies are born. Their home is in a hollow tree, with an entrance about ten feet above the ground; but to the four small, squirming, furry, black-masked babies it is warm and safe. They look exactly like their mother, except that their eyes are closed and they are very helpless.

When they are about three weeks old, their bright eyes open, but they stay in their nest, sucking warm milk, whimpering, sleeping, wriggling, and growing stronger. About the time they are a month old, they venture to the door of their home to look out at the forest which is their world. The young coons may wonder how they will ever get down to the ground from their door high up in the tree, and whether they should go head first or tail first. However, they stay in their nests until they are about two months old.

The great night comes at last, and when it is dark the mother raccoon looks everything over, just to be sure that it is safe to bring her youngsters out. Then they follow her down the tree and find that it doesn't matter at all whether they go head or tail first when they have such long fingers to help them. As this is their

19

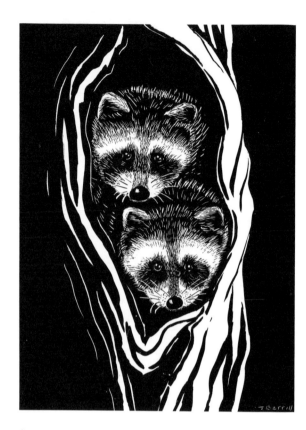

Young raccoons look out at the world

first trip to find food, the mother does not take them far from home but only leads them to the edge of a stream. Here they watch her wade in and turn over stones to find crayfish. They see her crack the shells of mussels and snails. She sloshes these tasty bits up and down in the water and then shares them with her wide-eyed youngsters waiting on the bank with excitement.

Each night they learn new and thrilling things by watching their mother, and while she slowly weans the young coons she teaches them the meanings of the sounds and smells of their forest world. Each night they travel a little farther from home; but they always return before the sun is up, to sleep all day, safe in their hollow tree.

4

Field Nurseries

RABBIT

The cottontail rabbit knows exactly when it is time to prepare a nursery and she hops about over the field looking for a suitable place. First she pokes her head into the shrubbery along the fence, then she inspects the spreading roots of a big oak tree, and still she is not satisfied. She hops over to a clump of grass and even starts to dig, but stops and looks about again. Finally she settles on a deep track made by a cow when the field was wet and soft.

By using this hole, her work is already partly done, and now she digs with her front paws until the hollow is about four inches deep, seven inches long, and five wide. It looks very much like a shallow bowl with its overhanging edges.

Mother cottontail's next job is to line the nest, and to do this she pulls soft hair from her breast and uses it, together with dry grass, until she has made the nest soft and warm.

Although she knew when to get the nest ready, she has no warning when the babies are about to arrive. More often than not she is away from home. If it is during the day, she will likely be hiding in the tall grass fast asleep; and if at night, she may be a hundred yards or more away, eating lettuce in the farmer's garden. So the babies may be born almost any place. She does not move them until they have had their first meal of warm milk;

then she takes them in her mouth, one at a time, and carries them to the waiting nest.

The cottontail mother does not stay with her babies all the time, for if she stays too close, she might attract the weasel or fox or eagle, her enemies, to the nest. She finds a spot close by where her gray-brown fur will blend with the grass and all day she keeps watch over her precious young.

To keep the babies warm while she is away all day, the mother makes a soft blanket of fur which she plucks with her teeth from the underside of her body and mixes with dry grass. When she is about to leave the nursery nest she carefully covers her babies with this blanket and then spreads leaves on top, so that they are really hidden as well as warm.

Since she does not return to her babies during the day, she only nurses them at night. They must be very hungry by sundown when their mother feels it is safe to go to them. She pulls back

A mother rabbit carefully covers her babies with a fur blanket

22

A young rabbit looks about

Bunnies wait quietly for their mother to return to the nursery

the coverlet and stands over the nest while they fill their little stomachs. She feeds them several times a night and after each nursing, she covers them well. She, too, must get her own food at night while the dark gives her some protection.

There are five babies in her litter, but there might have been as many as eight. They are blind at first, deaf, too, with tiny shriveled ears that lie flat to their heads. The very next day after they are born there is a fuzz all over them and at the end of a week they have beautiful, soft fur coats, complete with white fluffy tails. They can see and hear and their pointed ears perk up like their parents'. They are now stronger and can stand up and walk about a little.

After a couple of weeks they grow tired of their overcrowded home and spend some time each day outside, getting acquainted with the world about them. For the most part they sit quietly watching and listening, and smelling, too, with their twitching little noses. At night they return to the nest and curl up to keep warm and eat when their mother comes to nurse them. By the time they are sixteen days old, they are weaned and leave their nest for good.

5

Burrow Nurseries

CHIPMUNK

Many animals hide their nurseries underground; the chipmunk is one of these. These small creatures, looking like tiny squirrels with black stripes on their sides, are both shy and curious. They need rather soft soil in which to dig their homes and they push the loose dirt out of the hole with their noses and with their little paws spread wide at the sides of their faces. But the animals are clever and do not leave dirt by the door to tell all that pass that a chipmunk lives there. Sometimes it is smoothed out so you'd never guess; sometimes it is left in a pile, and the door plugged up and another entrance made under a rock or root of a tree.

Chipmunks are forever remodeling their homes, digging new storerooms or new tunnels. After a few years there may be twenty-five or more feet of tunnels and several different rooms. The toilet is always the lowest room in the burrow.

Most of you have seen chipmunks with their cheek pouches full, hurrying home to store the food. This storing goes on all year around. When the weather gets cold, the chipmunk works extra hard to fill the storage rooms, and when these are full, food is put in the bedrooms, under mattresses of grass and leaves. Each mattress gets higher and higher, with as much as half a bushel of seeds and nuts underneath, until it nearly reaches the ceiling.

When winter comes the animals curl up and go to sleep on these beds. When they become hungry, all they have to do is reach under the mattress and get some food. By spring the mattresses are back down on the floor!

About April the chipmunk babies arrive. There may be as many as four and they don't look like much of anything at all. They are very tiny, and you can almost see through them. They are blind, naked, and even their ears are closed. At first all they do is squeal, sleep, and drink their mother's milk. After two weeks they are covered with a fine fuzz and can stand on their wobbly little legs. By the time they are a month old their eyes are open and they look exactly like their parents, stripes and all. You may see them playing near the door to their underground home.

When summer ends the young chipmunks are big enough to leave their parents' home and dig burrows of their own.

WOODCHUCK

The woodchuck is a large, clumsy, slow-moving rodent that almost seems too heavy for its short legs. The fur is brown and coarse.

When winter comes the woodchuck, so fat from overeating that it can scarcely move, goes down into one of its underground bedrooms, at the end of a long tunnel, and closes the doorway with loose dirt. On the grass mattress, the creature rolls up into a ball, with its head between its legs, and drops into a deep sleep. There is barely any breathing, the heart hardly beats, and the body becomes stiff and cold—you would think it dead. This deep sleep is what we mean by hibernating.

All winter it lives on its stored fat, and when spring comes it is thin and hungry. When the ground is warmed by the spring sun, the woodchuck pokes its head out of its underground home.

The woodchuck babies arrive in the spring, usually four in a litter. They are helpless but know where to find good warm milk

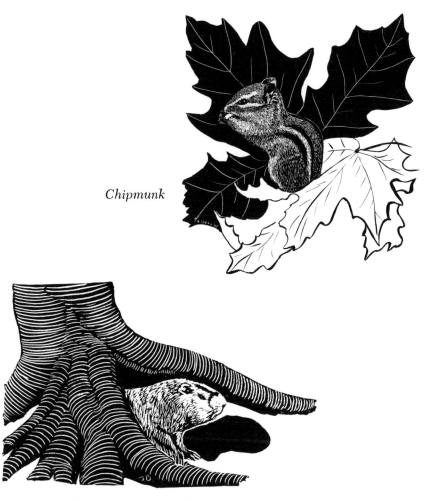

Chipmunk

A woodchuck peers out from its burrow

and very soon they begin to look like their parents. The mother keeps them very clean and often changes their soiled grass mattress for a fresh one of dried leaves.

After a month the babies begin to eat tender green plants which the mother brings to them. Soon they walk on their unsteady legs to the door of the den and eat new grass that grows nearby.

SKUNK

Skunks wear fur coats of three different patterns. One kind has a broad white stripe from head to tip of tail; another is black and white spotted; the other kind has two white stripes down the sides in a V design. No matter which coat is worn, they act the same when they are mad or frightened.

The skunk plays fair and gives plenty of warning that he means business. First he stamps his little feet several times; then he gives a low growl; but when he lifts his beautiful tail high, there is little time left in which to run, for without taking his eye from his enemy, he quickly twists into a U shape, with rear and face turned toward the intruder, and shoots out a thick, oily yellow liquid with its unmistakable odor. It may be a stream or a spray and it can land twelve feet away. The skunk doesn't invite trouble, but nature has given the creature this means of protection.

We find skunk homes along the borders of the woods, or in wooded ravines, or any place where there are lots of insects, for that is a favorite food.

Skunk mother entering her underground nursery to feed her babies

A skunk moves her baby to a safer nursery

The skunk living in my neighborhood wears a V-patterned coat and digs a burrow with the entrance well hidden under a bush. At the end of the tunnel, about two feet down, there is a bed room. To make the nursery warm and dry the female gathers dry leaves and grass and drags the pile beneath her body to the burrow entrance. Then she pushes the heap along with her head, down the tunnel and into the bedroom.

It is here that the tiny naked and helpless babies arrive in the early spring. There may be eight babies if the mother is old, or only three if it is her first litter. The black and white markings show under the thin skin even at first. The mother stands over them so they can nurse easily, but when they are larger, she lies on her side at dinner time.

They grow fast and soon wear fine coats marked like their parents'. The mother keeps her babies inside the burrow until they are six or seven weeks old and strong enough to follow her out at dusk to hunt food.

Since skunks sleep all day and hunt food only at night, we rarely see this delightful family. When we do, it is a night to remember—a mother headed toward a berry patch with her young following along in single file.

29

RED FOX

The red fox and his mate do not like to dig, so they hunt for an empty den made by another animal. An abandoned woodchuck burrow suits the pair well, for it is in the thicket, near a farm; also it is large and has many entrances. They clean it out well, enlarge some parts, and even make more tunnels if the ground is loose enough for easy digging, and move in.

The many entrances soon have well-beaten paths, that anyone can see, leading to them. The fox knows he can outwit most of his enemies and does not bother to hide his home as other woodland animals do. He depends on his keen intelligence and sharp eyes and ears for his protection.

The pair of foxes need a home only for a nursery during the early spring and summer; the rest of the year they sleep outside, curled up with their beautiful tails covering their long legs and faces.

The five fox babies—there might have been eight or nine—are born in the early spring and look exactly like puppy dogs. All they need is warm milk to help them grow fast, and the mother stays near to feed them often.

Red foxes are not always red, and this litter has one with a black coat. Another wears a reddish-brown one, with a black stripe down the back; the others are red like their parents. But all five have black legs, which makes them look as if they were wearing black stockings, and all have white-tipped tails.

When they are five weeks old the young foxes come out of the burrow to play in the sun around one of the entrances, with the parents on guard, of course. Never were creatures more beautiful than these fat balls of fur as as they roll over each other in their play.

All summer the father fox brings food to his growing young—

Fox cubs

meat, vegetables, and fruit—and on these they are weaned by the time the hot weather comes to an end. All fall the parents teach them to hunt food and to recognize their enemies, and by winter they can take care of themselves; that is, if they have learned their lessons well.

WOLF

You might have difficulty distinguishing a wolf from its close relative, the shepherd dog, but you would always be struck by the wolf's beauty. Physically they are perfectly adapted to living almost anywhere and taking care of themselves. Their noses are long and pointed and adept at picking up and following scent trails. Their ears are held high and do not miss a sound. The wolf is highly intelligent and seems to like to match its wits with man.

In the spring the female wolf selects an abandoned burrow and cleans it out, or she may dig a new one to her liking. Here, underground, she has her pups, sometimes as many as fourteen fluffy balls of fur with tightly closed eyes. After a week their eyes open,

31

but for about three weeks the mother scarcely leaves them, because they nurse much of the time and she stays near to watch over them and keep them warm. Her devoted mate hunts food and brings it to her, and she eats at the door of the burrow and returns quickly to her babies.

The pups grow rapidly. In half a year they are twenty-four inches high, and although they are fully grown at the end of a year, they do not leave their parents for two or three years. When the pups are about three months old the family leaves the den, not to return to it again but to roam together, very slowly at first until the young can travel far and fast. The wolf parents spend all their time teaching their young to hunt and to use their wits. The pups watch every move their parents make, for learning their woodland lessons will mean life or death to them.

Young wolf at the den entrance

Wolf

6

Cave and Rock Dens

TIGER

The cave home of the tiger family is at the head of a deep ravine where the heavy branches of trees and a tangle of vines completely hide the entrance. A large tiger, about the size of a lion, pushes aside the curtain of green leaves and steps out into the moonlight. He has dark, almost black, stripes on his fawn-colored coat. Silently, on his great massive paws, he walks over the soft fern-covered earth. He turns with a low growl toward the cave den as if to say, "What is keeping you? Come along!"

Almost at once the tigress, followed by three cubs, appears in the clearing. She is smaller than her mate, but just as beautifully marked. She is ferocious when guarding her cubs, yet she is an affectionate mother.

The cubs, now nearly a year old, jump about in the moonlight, playing like any kittens. They are glad to be out of the dark cave where they have been sleeping on and off all day, waiting for night to come so they can follow their parents along the quiet jungle path in search of food.

Often these tigers join other tiger families and hunt in groups, their loud growls helping them to keep in touch with one another. But sometimes the family hunts alone, for the cubs must learn much in the two years they are with their parents. They must learn to lie silently in the tall grass along the river, close to the

Tiger

place where other jungle animals come to drink, and to move quickly and with courage when the time arrives to take a long leap toward their prey. They must learn that their success in hunting depends upon this surprise pounce and not on trying to run after a fleeing antelope or other creature.

The tiger den served as a warm safe nursery when the cubs were born and it continues to be their home throughout their long growing period of two years while they learn to take care of themselves. Tigers are hunters and survival depends on learning their nightly lessons well. When daylight comes the tiger cubs, no longer hungry, follow their parents to the river to quench their thirst and then they proceed along the jungle path toward their cave. The excitement of the hunt has made them sleepy.

LION

All through the heat and the glare of the day the lioness has been lying asleep or nursing her cubs. Now she has other important business, that of getting food, for she is hungry. Already her mate stands growling at the entrance of their rocky den. She yawns, stretches, and moves out onto the path between the rocks to join him. The cubs rush forward, eager to follow her, but she turns and gives a low growl which sends them running to the safety of their den.

This rocky ledge along one side of the African plain is a perfect place for the lion family to live. Not far away is the water hole where herds of antelopes, zebras, and giraffes come to drink. Thorn bushes and tall grass grow along the banks of the river bed and, there hidden, the lion and lioness can usually be assured of a good dinner.

The lion is uncomfortable when out of his den in the daytime, for the pupils of his eyes stay round and wide open in sunlight,

Mother lion washes her cub at the entrance to the den

and do not contract to a mere slit as your pet cat's do. So his vision in the daytime is not very good and he is uneasy, but in the dark of the night he is really the "king of the beasts." Although it is not yet dark, the lions are hungry and they move restlessly about, their rich brown color blending perfectly with the sun-parched grass. The male, larger than the female, has a long mane which is darker than the rest of his coat. The lioness, more slender and graceful, has no mane but her hair is sleek and soft. Her movements are quick and very savage, now that she is a mother, and when she guards her young she is more to be feared than her mate.

Lions may hunt alone or in pairs, or sometimes several pairs unite to form a group that cooperates in hunting. Tonight this particular pair of lions stalk their prey. They move silently along until they reach a place near the water hole. The lioness remains quietly watching while the lion moves forward slowly, circling around the herd of antelope so as to get the wind at his back.

Lion

When the right moment arrives he roars loudly and the frightened animals scatter in the direction of his mate, who is hiding in ambush. When they come near enough she springs on the back of a young buck.

Now their dinner is secured and they set about to enjoy it. If they are weaning the cubs a part of the night's catch is taken back to share with the waiting young, who before long will accompany their parents on these nightly hunting trips, learning the ways of their kind. They do not kill for joy; they hunt only to live. Lion cubs have much to learn between the first months of their lives, when they play together happily and carelessly, and the

Lioness

time when they are on their own and must find their food for themselves and care for cubs of their own hidden away in a rocky den.

MOUNTAIN LION or PUMA

At the entrance of a rock cave in the hills the mother puma watches her three cubs as they play about, wrestling in the sun. This is a home among the rocks on a hillside, but it might just as well have been in the scrub bush on the plains or among reeds in a swamp, or even in desert lands. It could be in the north of Canada or on the southern tip of South America; almost any place in the Western Hemisphere would do for their home, for these large cats can adapt to all sorts of conditions and any safe place could be a nursery for the puma cubs.

They combine superb muscles, powerful jaws, strong claws, and a shyness which keeps them as far from man as they can get. The mountain lion, as the puma is called, wants only food and to be let alone.

The female cares for the cubs who are spotted dark brown on

Baby mountain lion or puma

40

a fawn-colored coat and look like kittens as they play and roll about on the ground. To the mother falls the responsibility of guarding them, as well as teaching them the rules of the wilderness. They will stay with her for nearly two years, learning all she can teach them.

These mountain lion cubs are but two months old, just old enough to follow their mother at dusk silently down the steep incline and along a rocky ledge overlooking a savannah where a herd of deer is grazing. She does not take them very far on their first trips, but the time will come when they will hunt over a twelve-mile range every night and return to sleep all day in their cave den.

The mother makes a perfect demonstration of how to stalk their prey, silently waiting and then crouching to spring on the back of the nearest deer. Her movements are swift and her aim precise, and the cubs rush forward so as not to miss a thing. Always before the mother had carried a piece of meat back to the cave for them to eat; now they taste their first warm meat fresh from the kill. This is such a new experience that they eat little but get very soiled and the mother washes each in turn. Afterwards she covers with brush the remains of the kill so she can return to it when she is hungry. Followed by the tired cubs, she pads softly away toward the cave where she nurses the babies until they fall asleep.

Before they are much older they will learn to spring from a tree, or to creep along in the slinking manner of all cats and wait for just the right moment to make a swift leap. They will watch their mother lead a pack of dogs on a chase and return safely because she outwitted her pursuers. These and many other things they will learn, but always they move silently along their way, with never a roar or a growl, only an occasional low hiss when they are angry.

41

Leopard sunning by his door

7

Pouch Nurseries

OPOSSUM

The female opossum, knowing it is time to get a nursery ready, searches out a deserted underground den or a nest in a hollow tree. With her grasping tail she carries into it bundles of clean dry grass and leaves. This is all for her own comfort, for the opossum has a very special pouch nursery, all fur-lined, in which the new babies, at first no larger than beans, finish their growth. Each baby possum must pull itself along the fur for about three inches to the opening of the pouch, on the underside of the mother, where it finds a nipple and hangs on. It is unable to suck so the mother pumps milk into it at nursing time for the next couple of months.

Now this really is a safe nursery, for wherever the mother goes she carries along her developing family. Before the babies leave the nursery for the first time the pouch almost touches the ground. When they finally leave the pouch they are about the size of mice and they cling to their mother's long scraggly back hair, or entwine their grasping tails about her tail. At night the young opossums return to the fur-lined pouch nursery to nurse and to sleep. By the time they can no longer fit in comfortably, they are weaned and can take care of themselves.

*Young opossums peek out
from their pouch nursery*

Opossum babies ride pickaback

KANGAROO

Australia is the home of all the other pouched mammals. Each drove of kangaroos has its own feeding grounds, and early in the morning and at twilight, one sees them eating vegetables, shrubs, heather, and grasses.

It is fun to watch kangaroos sitting about using their hind legs and tails like three-legged stools. With one push of their powerful hind legs they spring into the air, balance with their tails, hold their small front legs close to their bodies, and land—sometimes as far as twenty feet away, only to bound forward again and again.

Their strong hind legs, with their toe claws, are dangerous weapons in a fight; but kangaroos are really timid and shy and spend more time in the shade of tall bushes than they do fighting.

The single kangaroo baby is born like any other mammal baby —alive, naked, red, but only an inch long and very, very helpless. It has had only five weeks of growth in the mother's body and now it must make its way to a pouch on the underside of her body in order to continue growing. It uses its small front claws to pull itself, hand over hand, to the stomach pouch nursery. The mother licks a wet path for the blind helpless baby to follow, and at the same time keeps her stomach very straight and still. This is a most dangerous journey, because should the baby fall before it reaches the opening, it would die.

When it reaches the fur-lined nursery pouch, there is a teat ready for it, but the baby is so helpless it can't even suck. In fact, it doesn't even have enough strength to hold on, so the tip of the teat swells up, once it is in the baby's mouth, and then the mother forces milk down the baby's throat by contracting a muscle around the milk gland. She continues to feed it this way for three or four months, until the baby kangaroo is strong enough to suck when it is hungry.

Young kangaroo is almost too big for its nursery

Wherever the mother goes she carries the baby with her, safe and warm and fed. By the time it pokes its head out to look around, the cute little fellow looks like its mother. At first it just nibbles grass and leaves, when there's any nearby. Finally it hops out of the fur-lined baby carriage and walks along beside the mother. But it takes only a small, strange noise to send the youngster hurrying back, head first, to the safety of the nursery. Once inside, it turns quickly, and out comes the small head to see what happened, brave as anything now that it is safe!

KOALA

Australia is also the home of the koala bears, although they aren't bears at all, but pouched mammals like the kangaroo.

Koalas eat only the leaves of eucalyptus trees, and spend most of their lives a hundred and fifty to two hundred feet up, sitting on a limb, eating tender shoots. They seem especially made for tree life, with their strong claws and no tail to interfere with their climbing. Of course they sometimes fall out of a tree, but they land on their feet and climb right up the tree again.

Koalas are not fully grown until they are four years old, and they live to be about twenty. Every other year, the females have their young, usually just one, although sometimes there are twins. Like the other pouched mammals, the baby is very small, only three-quarters of an inch long, yet it manages to pull its way across thick fur to the opening of the pouch.

Once in the fur-lined nursery, it is safe and it sleeps and drinks and doesn't even peep out until it is about six months old. By then it has a beautiful fur coat like its mother's, the same bright eyes, and is seven inches long. For yet another couple of months the baby stays in the pouch, which finally becomes too small for comfort; then the youngster moves to its mother's back, where it

47

Koala young rides safely in the treetops

clings on for dear life. The fur of the mother is so thick it must be easy to cling to; at least the baby koala doesn't seem to be afraid when the mother climbs about on the branches high overhead.

The mother's back now becomes the nursery, and it is not unusual to see a baby nearly as large as the mother riding pickaback, or hugged close in the mother's arms while she warms it when they rest, sitting in the fork of a tree.

SEA HORSE

Mammals aren't the only creatures that have discovered the use of pouches for safe nurseries. No nursery is more strange than that of the sea horse, and in this case it is the male and not the female that has the pouch.

Eggs scattered in the sea drift away from the weeds which give young fish protection and among which will be found the food the young need when they hatch. When the female sea horse lays her eggs, they are fertilized by the male, who takes them at once into a brood pouch which he alone possesses.

The pouch of the sea horse is made of the two pelvic fins, and it holds several hundred eggs. For two months the eggs are perfectly safe, for the father carries them wherever he goes. When the time comes for the young sea horses to be set free, he twists his grasping tail about a bit of seaweed and bends his body backward and forward until they shoot out of his pouch, head first. It takes a long time for so many babies to leave their nursery. And for a long time they stay near enough to rush for the safety of the pouch nursery when they are frightened.

The male sea horse has the nursery pouch

8

Hang-on Nurseries

BAT

Bats are small mammals, too, the only ones that have wings and can really fly. They have no nursery nests and cannot leave their newborn babies hanging upside down in a dark cave, or at the top of a tree, while they go flying off to catch insects. So the mothers carry their babies wherever they go for about two weeks. The babies hang tightly to their mother's breasts, with their little claws clinging to the mother's fur, as she swoops through the air each night. All day long they hang upside down in the dark with their mother's wings folded about them for protection and warmth.

Above: Baby bat clings on tightly when mother goes out for food
Below: Bats hang asleep in the dark cave

SLOTH

Hanging upside down from a tree branch in the South American forest is one of nature's queerest creatures—the sloth. You would probably pass a sleeping sloth without seeing it, for it resembles a clump of green hanging moss. Its long fur is filled with tiny plants which, in the rainy tropics, flourish anywhere they can find a place to grow, and the fur of the slow-moving sloth is an ideal spot. However, they give the sloth a perfect protective camouflage, and animals searching for food during the day would never suspect the clump of moss was alive and edible.

When night closes in, the creature's small head lifts and her little eyes look about to find a choice bud or tender leaf. In a deliberate way she reaches one set of claws over the other as she progresses slowly along the branch, eating as she travels.

Hanging tightly to the fur on the underside of the female sloth is a small replica of its mother. There is no chance of being flung out of this slow-moving nursery and the contented baby nurses when it's hungry and sleeps the rest of the time. The small ball of fuzz has its sharp claws entwined in the mother's long fur, so is quite safe.

When the baby is larger you might even see it hanging upside down, clinging to the back of its upside-down mother. Where she goes, the baby goes until it is old enough to travel slowly along the limb. By this time enough plants are growing on its fur to make it resemble a clump of moss, too, as it hangs sleeping all day long.

MONKEY

The baby monkey lives in a "hang-on" nursery, too, for from the time it is born its hands cling tightly to the hair of its mother's chest. There is no other safe way. Of course the mother helps by

The baby sloth is happy in its upside-down nursery

Monkey baby is safely tended in the treetop nursery

cradling her beloved baby in one arm when it is first born. Later when it can hold on tightly enough she does not have to support it — but she is ever watchful and ready to help. She knows that one fall from their tree-top world would kill the baby, and so she is especially protective.

For many weeks the baby is scarcely out of her arms, for even when the monkey troop stops to rest the mother nurses her baby and carefully cleans its fur.

When the young monkey is older it travels pickaback, still holding tightly to the long fur on her back. When night comes the baby monkey is kept warm and secure, folded in her arms in the treetops.

9

Temporary Hideaways

WHITE-TAILED DEER

Where the sunlight filters through the hazel and willow trees, making light and dark patterns on the ferns that cover the forest floor, the fawn sleeps. It blends with its quiet woodland nursery; light polka dots on a reddish coat make it almost invisible.

The doe, the mother white-tailed deer, steps gracefully and silently to the side of the fawn, who stands up on its weak wobbly legs and nuzzles the mother. She stands, holding her head high, listening and watching as the baby nurses. When it is satisfied she licks its face and head, and then pushes it to the ground and moves out of the small clearing.

Fawn waits quietly in the thicket hideaway

When it is safe, the deer returns to feed her baby

She stays nearby watching, but not so close that she will attract enemies to her hidden nursery. The fawn has no strong
scent to give away its hiding place and so is safer alone. The
mother returns only to feed her infant, and each time the baby
is stronger and more restless. After two weeks it is strong enough
to leave the hide-away nursery and to travel about at night with
its mother, to visit the pond for a swim and the meadow for a
romp. The young deer stays close to her at first but slowly ven-
tures out to investigate its world. Any strange noise sends the
mother's white tail up as a warning and the fawn runs, with the
doe, to the shelter of the dense woods.

10

Nurseries on the Run

ZEBRA

Herds of zebras and antelopes graze peacefully on the grassy plain in the hot African sun. The ground is hard and level; a few willow trees and thorn bushes follow the curves of the dried up river bed.

The zebra's jet black stripes against pure white break the scene into lights and darks and give the right amount of camouflage. There are no outward signs of anxiety or even watchfulness. The zebras graze peacefully with their heads bent low and their eyes, placed far enough above their mouths, make it possible for them to watch and eat at the same time. Have you ever wondered why the horse and many other animals have long faces? They are all animals that, in their natural state, graze in open places where their safety depends on their seeing the wolf in time to run away swiftly on their long legs. They must therefore be able to crop the grass off near the ground and, at the same time, watch above the long grass for the approach of an enemy.

The plains animals can have no hidden nurseries. Their young must be able to follow with the herd as soon as they are born if necessary. A mother zebra stops grazing to nuzzle her nursing colt. His hair is long and shaggy but his camouflage stripes are like hers and were so even when he was born the week before over in the thorn thicket by the river bed. All week the mother

Young zebra never wanders far from its mother

and colt had stayed out of sight as much as possible so that the colt's legs could grow stronger before they joined the herd. Had there been no thicket the zebra would have had to run along by the mother from the first. However, his legs, like those of all colts, are now long, and occasionally he kicks up his hoofs to show just how strong he has become in this one short week.

Zebra

From now on he will take his place in the herd whose only home is the wide open land. Like all zebras he is timid and shy and easily alarmed, and even starts up ready to run when he hears a slight movement near a group of trees. But it is only a family of giraffes browsing daintily on the top leaves of a tree. Instinctively he knows that no harm will come to him from these strange long-necked creatures and so, ignoring them, he snuggles close to his mother again.

The zebras and giraffes and antelopes all have long slender legs, especially adapted for speeding over open ground. This is their chief defense. However, they know that their strength lies in keeping together in a compact group.

GIRAFFE

The large male leads the giraffe herd across the grassland with an ungainly walk which is the result of moving both legs on one side at the same time. The females, shorter than the males, move more slowly so as to allow their young calves to keep up with them. When they reach a group of acacia trees they are almost invisible, for they have white markings over their orange-red coats, and their heads, nineteen feet in the air, are lost in the tops of the trees.

It is hard to accept giraffes as real living flesh and blood creatures; they seem so lifeless, as if they were stuffed with straw. Yet here on the African plains they live on peaceful terms with their own kind and with other animals, and they move about in herds guarded by their leader. Because of their towering height

Giraffe has difficulty reaching the water

Mother and young travel close together

they have few enemies and are only occasionally attacked by a lion, who must be very hungry to risk being killed by the powerful kick of an angry giraffe.

Giraffes have large brown eyes that are placed in such a way that they can see what goes on behind as well as in front of them. They have long tongues that can be used like a far-reaching hand and, besides this, they possess special nostrils that can close

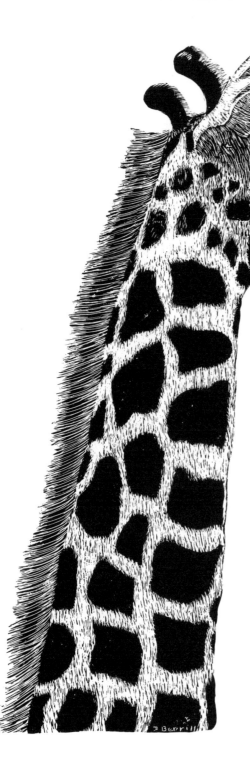

tightly when the air is full of wind-blown sand.

A young giraffe calf finishes nursing and wanders a few feet away to investigate the strange black and white creatures standing in the shade of a tree. But his mother tosses her head and snorts a warning, and he trots back to her side. Like the zebra colt, he and his mother have just returned to the herd, for he was born near an outcropping of rocks, where he and his mother remained until he could move fast enough to follow her about.

Giraffes do not go to the water hole for a drink any oftener than they have to because they realize

Kudu antelope

they are helpless when they spread their legs wide enough apart for the long necks to reach the cool water. It is small wonder they dread the ordeal, but as soon as they have quenched their thirst they break into a stiff gallop, looking more like rocking horses than real animals.

How did these unbelievable animals come to look like this? Giraffes got long legs the better to speed across the plains away from their enemies. As their legs grew lengthier their shoulders got farther from the ground but they still had to reach grass and water — so the neck had to stretch longer and longer. Once the giraffes had long necks, it became no longer necessary to eat grass all the time, for they could now reach the leaves on trees and so became browsers instead of grazers and hold their heads higher than any other animals.

ANTELOPE

Many herds of antelope graze on the broad plains, too. Each has its own special kind of markings, as well as its own shape of horns, and those which are alike stay together. All antelopes have long slender legs and, like the zebra and horse, their eyes are placed far enough above their mouths so they can watch and graze at the same time. They are always alert and run at the least disturbance, for they know that behind every thorn bush a lion may be waiting. The young antelopes stay close to their mother's side and all feel safety in being close together as they graze.

So you see that plains animals have no real hidden nurseries. At best, a bush or a rock may give slight and brief shelter at the time of birth and for a few hours afterwards while the wobbly legs grow strong enough to hold the baby upright. But when the herd moves on to better grazing the antelope baby walks along by its mother's side to join the others of its kind. Alone on the plains they could not survive.

Index

Jacquelyn Berrill

was born in Kentucky, graduated from the University of Toledo, and did post graduate study at New York University. She was a group social worker with teen-age girls in the Jackson and Lansing, Michigan, Y.W.C.A. before her marriage to Dr. N. J. Berrill, zoologist, author, and professor.

The Berrills have three grown children and now two granddaughters old enough to enjoy their grandmother's books. Besides keeping house and writing and illustrating her books, Mrs. Berrill is interested in many arts and crafts, including ceramics, jewelry, painting, and batik, her newest hobby.